MEDITATIONS TO LIVE BY:
Attuning to the Power of Love

Joyce A. H. Ellenbecker

Judie Arbess Diamond

Copyright © 2017 Ellenbecker & Diamond

All rights reserved.

For Jim Wellemeyer, teacher, mentor and friend.

For Milo Jonah Nam Diamond Fong, hope for the future.

Contents

Introduction 1
   A Word from Joyce 1
   A Word from Judie 3
Credits 5
How to use this book 6
Beginnings 8
   Breathing Meditation 9
   ABC Meditation: Align, Breathe, Connect 11
   Morning Meditation: A Balancing Act 14
   Acceptance Meditation 16
Oneness 18
   Return to Oneness 20
   Oneness of Being 24
   Reverence for Life 28
Wisdom 31
   Saints Among Us 32
   Living, Loving, Learning 36
   Seeing Connection 39
   Body Wisdom 43
Peace 47
   Peace in Every Heart 48
   Sun Shine On Me 51
   Peace Within, Peace Without 52

Serenity	56
Seeing Clearly	**59**
Freedom from Attachment	60
Natural Rhythms	63
Sanctification	66
Joy, Appreciation, Self-Love	67
Remembering Our Creativity	69
Trust in the Flow	72
Body Field	**76**
Chain of Pearls	77
Rainbow Meditation	82
Re-sourcing	85
The Aramaic Lord's Prayer	88
Field of Flowers, Field of Love	89
Grounding	**93**
Still Meadow Trees	94
Hand Attunement	99
Feet on the Ground	103
Walking Meditation	108
Appendix	**110**
History of Attunement	111
Endocrine Glands and Associated Spirits	113
Annotated Bibliography	**117**
Biographies	**120**
Acknowledgements	**122**

Photographs:

Front cover   Walk to the Beach
Back cover   Sunset at Diamondhead

Introduction

A Word from Joyce

It is always interesting to me how a book originates. This one started a few years ago, even before I knew it was going to be written. I was introduced to Attunement in the 1970s through a spiritual group called the Emissaries of Divine Light. I shared Attunement with others and then started to teach it in 1999. I wanted people to have a greater experience of Attunement, therefore I started Attunement circles in people's homes.

One of those circles was in Laguna Beach, California. The person whose home we were meeting in decided to move and we were not able to continue in the same way. It was at that time we decided we would share Attunement by phone once a month. A conference line was set up and the meditations were recorded. Later, I had them transcribed, as a teaching opportunity for me. It was at this point that the idea of a book was born. I contacted different friends to see if they would give me feedback and help with editing. Judie Diamond offered to do a first edit and said she would like to collaborate. The collaboration with Judie has been exciting and opened a whole new learning experience.

When we share a meditation, there is a feeling of wholeness, relaxation and peace. The meditations in this book are based in the cosmology of Attunement, which, like meditation, chant and prayer, recognizes that we are more than just our physical body. We have an energy body, also known as an aura, subtle or etheric body. In Attunement, we call it pneumaplasm. It is not necessary to be familiar with the practice of Attunement in order to benefit from these meditations.

Attunement is a spiritual practice uniting body, mind and heart with Spirit. We become aware that we are connected to something more than just ourselves, it can be called the universal life force, Source or God. I like to believe that we are angelic beings having a human experience. Our nature is to be whole in body, mind and spirit: as this happens, there is an aspect of healing that is able to take place at whatever level is needed.

A Word from Judie

I have been wanting to write an Attunement-based book forever! I was thrilled when Joyce accepted my offer to share some of my Attunement meditations here. It has been a wonderful experience working with Joyce to bring the book to fruition.

I "met" Attunement in 1981 and was literally struck by it while watching a demonstration at a seminar in a Montreal hospital. I didn't know if I believed in signs, but this was surely one! I quickly began studying and pretty soon, practicing, first on family and friends. This developed into teaching and facilitating Attunement in circles, gatherings, classes, retreats and personal sessions, mostly at our country home in rural Ontario. From 1997-2006, I served on the Leadership Group of the Attunement Guild, with Joyce as a collaborator and friend.

Seven years ago, I was asked to start a regular teleconference with some kind of group attunement and came up with the name: Sharing Attunement Frequency Elevation Teleconferences. The acronym, SAFE Calls, soon took hold. These hour-long calls have continued ever since on a monthly basis. I have not recorded them: the meditations are generally written within 24 hours of the calls.

Attunement is a practice in the fullest sense. Although there are techniques that can be used to great advantage, it is the commitment to an attunement-based lifestyle that really works. I think of Attunement as the space of love and truth. In Attunement, we learn to "follow the energy." There is so much complexity in personal and global events, so much to distract and discourage. We cannot avoid these challenges, they are an integral part of the human condition, like it or not. What we can do is put our attention on the higher and finer stimuli that are available. "Where attention goes, energy flows", another energy principle worthy of repeating. The meditations in this book are born out of this quality of intention and attention.

Whether using one's hands to connect with another's energy field or sharing a guided meditation, there is a shift in the energetic field of the participants, a freeing up of energy that has in some way been bound up and is seeking release. As several of the meditations remind us, energy is meant to move in, through and out of our fields in a continuous flow. One of my friends recently described it as a "hands off, consciousness on" practice.

CREDITS

Photos for front & back covers by Joyce Ellenbecker
Dolphins by Minako Hata Ellenbecker
Joyce's photo by Wendy Crosman
Judie's photo by Adriana Palanca
All other photos by Joyce Ellenbecker
Book front & back cover designed by Jackson Logan
Poem "New Bearings" by Diana Durham
Poem "Sanctification" by Louise Broomberg
Poem "Morning Meditation" by Judie Diamond
Song "Sun Shine on Me" by Judie Diamond
Aramaic Lord's Prayer, translation by Neil Douglas-Klotz
First edit by Judie Diamond
Final edit by Adriana Palanca
Publishing Coordinator, Laurence Layne

How to use this book

When we hear the word "meditation", it can bring many different meanings to mind. In this book, we invite you to use meditation to quiet the mind and allow the life force to move through your bodies, minds and hearts, to listen to what your body and your life have to say. This promotes relaxation, sharpens awareness and allows the body to come into a natural state of well-being.

There is no right way to engage with these meditations. Here are some suggestions which may serve to enhance your experience. Find a quiet place where you can relax. Take time to read each meditation. You may want to read silently or out loud. You can use the meditations alone or share them in a group. While reading, pause to allow the words to resonate. You will see the word "breathe", take the time to do so. You will find a rhythm that is comfortable for you. It is during the pauses that the energy has a chance to move. Let it!

You can read consecutive chapters and meditations as they are ordered, or simply open the book to a page and trust that this is the message you need at the moment. If images come up for you that differ from the images given, go with your experience. Likewise, Spirit, Source, Life, God and Love all refer to the same energy. Choose the one that best resonates with you.

Although these meditations were originally spoken during teleconferences, the energy that was generated is maintained and conveyed whenever the words are spoken or read. In the conversion to the written word, we may have made shifts in pronouns or tone.

The book has been divided into chapters. The meditations in each chapter follow a theme.

The chapter called Grounding includes some specific techniques. There are two meditations using the skeletal system, one using the hands and the final one is a walking meditation. More explicit directions are given within each meditation.

The appendix has a more complete description of Attunement and the endocrine glands.

Enjoy.

BEGINNINGS

Breathing meditation

We all breathe every living moment of our lives. Today, I am going to ask you to breathe consciously, to be aware of your breathing.

Close your eyes. Become aware of your breath.
Breathe in, breathe out. Be aware of your breath.
Don't try to control it. Just notice, be aware.

Breathe.

Do you hold your breath or pause while you're breathing?
Do you pause after you breathe in?
Do you pause after you breathe out?
Are your breaths continuous, without pauses?
Be aware.

Breathe.

Where do you feel the breath?
Do you breathe in the upper part of your lungs only?
Do you belly breathe?

Breathe.

Do you breathe slowly and rhythmically?
Are your breaths shallow or deep?

Breathe.

Envision yourself running.
Does your breathing change?

Breathe.

Imagine that you see someone you love.
Does your breathing change?

Breathe.

Breathe in, breathe out.
Be aware of your breath.

Breathe.

As you come out of the meditation, begin to move around and gently open your eyes.

JE

ABC meditation: Align, Breathe, Connect

Here is a meditation I use frequently to ground myself and to assist my friends to ground and center. I call it the "ABC meditation", because it follows an alphabetical pattern. It's easy to remember if you are interested in exploring meditation on your own.

A — Align
Focus your attention inward, on the position and alignment of your body. Allow your body to find a posture that is erect, yet relaxed, with your spine slightly elongated. Place your feet flat on the floor or earth, bring your attention to the bottoms of your feet and notice the sensation of making contact with the ground. Imagine that there is an energetic opening in each foot, and breathe through these openings, bringing fresh, nourishing energy up from the earth into your body.

B — Breathe
As you align your body in this way, a natural breath may follow, one that is deeper and fuller than usual. Focus on the breath coming up through the midline of your body, up from the earth through the tailbone and up the spine to the head, up to the top and out, through the crown, like the blowhole of a whale. On the out-breath, follow the same pathway through the midline and allow the air to exit through the tailbone.

C — Connect
Feel into your connection with a larger energetic space,

with the universal whole. Allow your subconscious to offer a word, a phrase, an image or thought-form that leads you to discover (or recover) another state of awareness, an expanded state. This is a higher-vibration reality that always exists but that we rarely access. Regular practice facilitates the ability to connect with this powerful, yet gentle space. Align. Breathe. Connect.

Although it is not necessary to continue the meditation using consecutive letters of the alphabet, here are a few suggestions that may work for you or may encourage you to develop your own structure.

D — Discover
Feel into this expanded reality, discover where you now "are". Allow your awareness to go where it goes and simply notice what is transpiring in your body, in your thoughts, in your feeling sense. When you are in this expanded space, another level of attention emerges, embodying wisdom and guidance for you. Listen.

E — Exhale
On the in-breath, allow clear, fresh energy to come into the body, into the mind, into the heart. Reach for the new energy that is waiting to nourish your body. On the out-breath, allow yourself to let go of bodily tension, mental stress, emotional turmoil. Exhale any stagnant energy that is lingering, any old information that is no longer needed.

A purer, clearer energy field supports your daily rhythmic cycle. You become more aware of a healthy balance between activity and rest.

F — Free up energy
The process of meditation, of being in attunement with something greater than our ordinary selves, allows energy that is no longer needed in the body to be freed up and to move on. One of the principles of energy work is that energy is meant to move in, through and out. This is what is referred to as "being in the flow."

Breathe. Let go. Feel the flow of energy through you.

G — Be grateful
Gratitude is the anchor of virtually every spiritual practice. Meditating on the word gratitude, thankfulness or appreciation is beneficial in many ways. Bringing to mind or making a list of things we appreciate creates a healthy environment in the psyche. A gratitude journal can be a potent resource for strengthening a positive state of mind. Focus on gratitude. Breathe.

Closing Balance

Breathe in love.
Breathe out gratitude.
Breathe in gratitude.
Breathe out love.

These, along with joy and peace, are the highest and finest emotions for enhancing our health and well-being.

JD

Morning meditation: a balancing act

June 1st
New month
New day
New moment
    (Hope springs eternal)

Life instructs:
Use the four forces
To find your perfect balance

Water

Wetlands water shimmers in the early morning sun
Rippling from the movement of the creatures therein
Evoking clarity and true essence

Air

Wind, wending its way through the trees brings spirit
Birdsong accentuating gifts of the air

Earth

Earthly creations:
Ancient rock of granite and limestone
Horsetail lining the path, upturned leaves reaching
Poplars and maples in abundance
One lone leaf catches my full attention
Revealing itself to me, naked and unashamed
Touches my heart

Fire

Sun beams down on all its dependents, warming,
nurturing
Providing energy, strength, all that is needed
To allow each one of us
To rest.

JD

Acceptance meditation

Many of the meditations in this book follow a particular structure. Both authors are steeped in the cosmology and practice of Attunement, a spiritual energy-healing practice that is based in the endocrine system. There are seven endocrine glands and, in Attunement, each gland represents a particular focus of spirit. We begin with an initial balance of the entire energy field, then attune each gland starting at the top with the pineal and proceeding gland by gland, spirit by spirit.

Opening balance
I ponder these questions: What is needed in this moment? What does Spirit intend? Today one word comes to awareness: restfulness.

Spirit of Love (pineal gland)
I focus on the Spirit of Love. Images pop up of crystals, pale green and pink quartz. Gentle, loving energy. Very high frequency energy. Refined substance. Breathe in this rarefied air. Focus on the Spirit of Love. Accept what comes. Breathe.

Spirit of Truth (pituitary gland)
As I focus on the Spirit of Truth, essences come to awareness: restfulness, protection, loving, nurturing. A womb-like context. A garden in which the true patterns of being can grow. A crystal chamber where all excess is filtered out and only what is true remains. Focus on the Spirit of Truth. Accept what comes. Breathe it in.

Spirit of Life (thyroid gland)
As I focus here, love and truth pass through and are magnified. Vibrant life abounds, expresses, communicates, articulates, bringing love and truth into the atmosphere in which it exists, bringing hopefulness, possibility of fulfillment. Breathe in the Spirit of Life. Let it fill you.

Spirit of Purification (thymus gland)
Focusing here evokes cleansing, clearing, protecting, defending, allowing pure self to be aware of itself and of what does and does not belong. Knowing with assurance and strength who I am and why I am here. Pure enjoyment of life — acceptance of all that life offers, all of it without judgement. Pure acceptance. Breathe in the Spirit of Purification. Let it move through you.

Spirit of Blessing (pancreas)
I open to the Spirit of Blessing, welcome the energy of being blessed and let that spirit pass through me, leaving complaint on the cutting room floor. Receiving light, radiance, assistance, support and love. Bringing more light, radiance, assistance, support and love. Breathe in the Spirit of Blessing, receive what comes, allow it in and through, offer it out. Breathe. Bless.

Spirit of the Single Eye (adrenal glands)
Although there are two adrenal glands, there is one focus: Spirit. As focus is singular and clear, stress magically evaporates, vanishing into thin air. Feelings of being confused or overwhelmed simply do not exist in

your awareness. Worry does not get the job done (any job), give it up!

Creativity predominates in each moment, all energy and attention given to the one point of focus: the present moment. All is well. Focus. Direct your attention to the activity of the moment. Give it your all. Only one moment exists. NOW. Breathe.

Spirit of the New Earth (gonads)
Newness, renewal, fresh energy from Mother Earth, gifts abounding. Let go of old stagnant energy, thoughts, feelings, concepts and see! What's here now? What is actually manifesting? What does God need me to understand? To know? To say? To do?

Listen and know. And act on the direction given — this is spiritual direction. Breathe it in. Follow it.

Closing balance
Balance, integration, wholeness, integrity, oneness. Connectedness. Easy flow of life. Be curious and open to the next moment while being fully in this moment. Be fulfilled: there is nothing but this. This is the life I am meant to live. I claim it. I live it. Nothing gets between my life and me. This is my pact with Source. Simply this: that I will live. Fully live!

JD

ONENESS

Return to oneness

I sit with the question; how much love can I know? How much love is possible? How deeply, how fully, can I experience love? When I am with my grandson or when I think about moments with him, I feel a physical sensation in my chest, along with a wave of emotion that often brings tears to my eyes. This has raised the question in me: how much love can I experience?

Opening balance
I place my attention inward. I open my energy channels to allow an expansion to occur, feel the life current flowing more vibrantly, more fully, more freely. I allow my energy to seep downwards, so that my center of gravity lowers, my awareness of the chair bottom intensifies, even as I feel the energy continuing downward... downward. I feel my breath deepening, my chest expanding on the in-breath, a prolonging of the out-breath. I am aware of a balance, a symmetry, a centeredness, a groundedness that is unusual in my daily experience.

Love
I focus on the word "love", on the spirit of love, somewhere above the crown of my head, opening to allow this energy to enter through my pineal portal. I breathe in these precious, refined vibrations. I breathe in, out, slowly, deeply, in full awareness of each sensation. The coolness of the breath as it passes my throat, the moment of exchange, the release of breath, release of tension on the out-breath.

Truth
I honor this moment, realize its uniqueness, appreciate its potential, welcome its offerings. I open to the very now, never before and never again to be. I vow to be with it and with each moment I am privileged to live, knowing my awareness will wane, but knowing too that I can return, and return, and return. Now. Now. Now.

Life
Life moves. Life is ever moving, moving towards the fulfillment of itself. In truth, in life, I am never stuck, only refusing to move in ways I don't like. Would that I remember that when I feel stuck! It's an illusion. No wonder I feel disillusioned. No! Open to the flow. Let life flow. In Attunement, we call it the current. The current of life.

"Current" has another meaning, referring to what's happening now. And what's happening now is life moving. Let it move. Why do things get stuck in my body, I wonder? Could it be related to damming (up) the flow? And, if I remove the walls, the dams, the barriers, the blocks, what happens then? Life keeps on moving, "That ole man river, he jest keeps rollin' along..."

Purification
This feels like a prayer. A prayer of purification. A purification prayer. Dear God, let my heart be purified. Let my mind be informed by Higher Mind, not addicted to my wants and long-held beliefs. May I allow what needs to pass through to pass through, in every way, thoughts, beliefs, desires, foods, tears... everything. May I allow energy in all its forms to flow in, through and out.

Blessing
"Praise God from whom all blessings flow." Let go and let God. Attune, commune with the great spirit of Love. Blessings in, blessings out. The secret is: every moment is a blessing, every moment! This air I breathe, is it not a blessing? This body I inhabit, knowing as it does how to take air in and breathe it out, moment by moment, hour by hour, day by day, year by year, is this not a miracle? Feel blessed now. And now. And now. And, if I am blessed, am full to overflowing, can I help but allow blessings to pour forth from my being? Breathe. Blessings in, blessings out.

Single Eye
The single eye is the moment of now, the ever-changing moment of now. Now. Now. Now. Now. Now. Now. Now. Nothing else exists in each moment. And yet they flow together, the moments, and merge into a coherent whole, seamless and elegant. I am focused, alert yet relaxed, aware of the whole yet only of what is at hand. I breathe. I see. I know. I am.

New Earth
Such riches await. No thing is necessary to awaken my interest, to stimulate my appetites, to satisfy my desires. It's all here. It's all now. Awaiting, doing, appreciating is all here now. No before and after, no during. It's been said before (is there a "before?") it's all here. Be here now. Live. Love. Be. There's nowhere to go, nothing to do, no one to see. It's all here, now. One foot in front of the other. One moment lived, then another. I guarantee another moment will present itself!

Closing balance

Breathe. Be. There is a power in being present, in allowing the moment to be as it is, in being willing to listen and hear the voice that speaks. Breathe as one. We are One. I am you and you are me. There is no separation. Let the illusion go once and for all and be in Love. This is where we meet. This is where we merge. It is good to return to the oneness of Love.

JD

Oneness of being

Here we are on Valentine's Day — an occasion we can use as a symbol of love — although perhaps not in the way Hallmark intended! Let's open our hearts to universal love and breathe together.

Spirit of Balance
Allow your world to come into balance. Allow your internal world to come into balance, by breathing in, breathing out. Allow yourself to come to a point of peace and ease.

Breathe.

Hold your hands about six inches apart and imagine holding your entire world of connection and influence in an energetic ball. Allow whatever wishes to be present to simply be there. Trust and allow.

Breathe.

Spirit of Love
Move to the Spirit of Love, the Spirit of Love that we all inherently are. We are creator-beings, we radiate love into all that we do and all that we are. We watch over our worlds in the Spirit of Love.

Breathe.

Spirit of Truth
Move into the Spirit of Truth. Be aware of the perfection

that we each are, the perfection of the Attunement process, the perfection that you bring through the Spirit of Love that is tempered with the Spirit of Truth and Wisdom in you.

Breathe.

Spirit of Life
We move into the Spirit of Life, the radiance of life. We see our world with all its beauty. We see limitations as an opportunity for the expression of wisdom and truth. We breathe life into our worlds.

Breathe.

Spirit of Purification
Move into the Spirit of Purification. As your thoughts and expression are clear, that which is in the heavens above can be expressed into your world, into the earth. You know the frequencies of love and perfection; you can express them into your world. That all things may be made new. That the chaos you find around you cannot disturb you, infuse it with your love of life.

Breathe.

Spirit of Blessing
Move into the Spirit of Blessing. You are blessed with knowing the perfection of your love. You are blessed as you give expression to the love that you feel with others. This is one of the blessings — the capacity to show appreciation, gratitude and love for others and for your

world.

Whatever the current hype may be around Valentine's Day, it's good to let others know you care, to extend the vibration of blessing to those around you.

Breathe.

Spirit of the Single Eye
Move to the Spirit of the Single Eye, knowing that you focus your own creative field and yet, you are connected to all, to the oneness of being, to the oneness that is everlasting, ever was and ever will be. It is a privilege to express through these physical beings in this time and place. What you bring into focus in your creative field is in harmony with others.

Breathe.

Spirit of the New Earth
Move into the Spirit of the New Earth. You bring into expression all of those spirits we've been evoking, of love, truth, life, purification, blessing and the single eye. You bring those qualities into consciousness and on through into the earth, knowing we are all one and that we bear witness to each other and to the perfection that we each are. You bear witness to your own perfection and to the perfection of others and to the oneness of life.

Breathe.

Closing balance

Give great thanks for each of us being our perfect selves and for agreeing to join in this unified radiation. Thank you.

JE

Reverence for life

Having a two-year-old in my life has heightened my sense of true living. With him, every moment is vibrant and exciting; a time for discovery, exploration, learning and doing. His total participation in everything he does, his obvious appreciation for all of life and reverence for life in such an innocent way! And I share that reverence.

Love
It's all about attention. Where is my ear attuned, to what am I listening? Can I shift out of my usual perspective and listen in an entirely different mode, being open to a vast range of vibrations, to the infinite possibilities that are available? It is a matter of choice, of conscious choosing. You'd think it would be easy to listen to love, to listen for love to speak, to reveal its wonders. But it isn't! There are so many distractions. Can you listen now to the clarion call of love, always present, always available, always accessible? It's your choice: choose love now!

Truth
Truth is the Way, the Tao, the path and the destination. Finding our Way, with a capital W! What is the truth of my way? Wouldn't I like to know! To have it all mapped out. But that's not how it works. Life is a constant series of transitions. And each moment of transition depends on the choice I made a moment ago. We do have free will in that sense, the freedom to choose. I have agency, power and the responsibility to be alert and poised for action, to choose to bring the best that I

can to this moment and trust that all is well, no matter what will follow.

Life
What a gift life is. Being alive. We have a strong tendency to take life for granted. No matter how much we aspire to be in an appreciative mode, we still have moments when we feel cynical and complain. And maybe that's fine. Maybe accepting ourselves with this tendency is part of balancing out the dark with the light!

Purification
Can we let our hearts be purified, each one of us? Can we allow ourselves to return to the innocence of childhood, with total participation in all of life's wonders, the dreary and the drab, the worry and the pain, the wonder and the joy? The whole range. The gamut! I know there is a point of balance in it all. The whole is greater than the sum of its parts. All of life's offerings are a necessary part. There's nothing wrong. We didn't get it wrong! Everything is as it should be. This brings to mind, "No doubt the universe is unfolding as it should." What do I know in the face of universal unfolding?

Blessing
There are many blessings. And there is ONE BLESSING. Let us share in that one blessing now. Let's merge with it so there is no distinction between giving and receiving. We are, individually and collectively, one with the One. Blessed and blessing. One state. One flow.

Single Eye
Here is the Spirit of the Single Eye in action. Is there good and bad here? Is there dark and light? Is there you and me? The term, "unified radiation" comes to mind. Feel it in your heart. A song pops into awareness, one that many of us know from early childhood: "The more we get together, together, together. The more we get together, the happier we'll be."

New Earth
And the New Earth emerges. Here it is! This is it! It's the actual experience of oneness, of no separation. The Way it's supposed to be. The Way it is.

Closing balance
Bless you for your time, your attention, your love and devotion, for who you are and everything you do.

JD

WISDOM

Saints among us

We've just celebrated Halloween and All Saints Day, and Thanksgiving is fast approaching. Tapping into the meaning of these three days, we can include in our meditation an acknowledgement of those in our past who have had a positive influence on us, and be thankful for them — to see them as saints in our lives. If anybody from your past comes and "joins you" at any time during the meditation, give them a blessing and let them move on.

Opening balance
Let's take a deep breath and come into the spirit of balance. This is the time of year when we're moving from a season of heavy activity into a season of quiet. There is a stillness in the wintertime, yet it is heralded by much activity during Thanksgiving, Christmas and New Year's. Allow yourself to come to rest while we have these moments together, while the moon is waning from full to new, signaling that a time of activity is transitioning into quiet.

Spirit of Love
The Spirit of Love is the life force from which we are created and incarnate into these bodies. Love energy enters through the pineal as undifferentiated energy, the wholeness of being. Let's breathe in the force of love and breathe out love.

Spirit of Truth
We move into the pituitary, into the Spirit of Truth, the

first differentiation of love. As we access the wisdom deep within us, those essences begin to differentiate into our true nature, our unique being. We breathe in truth and breathe out wisdom. The truth of who we are. The wisdom that we bring into our world.

Spirit of Life
We move into the Spirit of Life through the thyroid, where further evolution takes place. More refinement of the essences that we bring into our worlds: our talents, our insights, our unique assets, our expression. We breathe in the life force, breathe out our essences, those particular characteristics that we are designed to bring into the world.

Spirit of Purification
We move into the thymus; the Spirit of Purification comes through that beautiful gland of protection. We allow the purity of who we are to infuse our world. We welcome the protection the thymus gland provides for us through the immune system. We allow the specific vibrations from the heaven of who we are to flow through us, into the earth, into form.

We breathe in the purity of life and breathe out the assurance of our being, the assurance that we are making our unique contributions in an accurate way.

Spirit of Blessing
We move into the Spirit of Blessing, revealing those true essences that we are here to bring. Our purpose is to bless everything in our worlds, to bless those around

us, to bless ourselves. Let's come into the realization that we are creator-beings, that we each have something to offer, that we bring the life force that created us and the specific forms it takes in us. We bless our various talents, abilities and essences, those in ourselves and those in others. We bring into the world the blessings it so longs for.

Spirit of the Single Eye
We move into the Spirit of the Single Eye, the singleness of purpose, to bring the love essence into our worlds, while knowing that we are part of the singularity, the oneness of all. We are connected with each other, we are connected to the all, yet each of us is unique. Only you can bring that uniqueness. Only through our uniqueness do we bring the diversity of the Spirit of Love into the world. Through our diversity, we bring peace. Each of us radiates the peace that comes through us, that magnifies and that expands.

Spirit of the New Earth
We come to the Spirit of the New Earth, where each of us can express our full selves in creative ways. We learn how to blend with others and still remain true to ourselves, so that our talents, our love, our song can be known. We do that through blessing, gratitude, forgiveness and allowing ourselves to be creative in whatever ways are accurate for us.

Closing balance
We recognize our own gifts and we recognize the gifts of others. We are drawn to be with those who sing in

harmony with us. There may be times when there's a discordance, but that's an invitation to move into something more harmonious! That is how we bring the music of the spheres into this earth. Moving into harmony requires stillness, patience, listening and action, in union with others, so we may stand together, sing together, blessing our worlds, in balance and in harmony…

Prayer: We give great thanks for the opportunity to be together in this way, grateful that when we part company we go into our separate worlds aware that we are connected to something larger, and that we bring something of value with us. May the blessing of love be with you always. Amen.

JE

Living, loving, learning

As I sit quietly and focus within, the question arises: what is most needed in the world, in each of our worlds and in the world at large? The answer that comes into awareness: balance. And what is balance? The point on the teeter-totter where you don't actively move up or down, but are perfectly poised on a horizontal plane. Not very real in my experience! We are always transitioning to a new point, towards achieving, maintaining or sustaining equilibrium. There is continuous movement: physically, mentally, emotionally, spiritually.

Opening balance
Let's meditate on balance, harmony, equilibrium restored, stability. Let's bring that state of balance into our experience now: for ourselves, for each other, for our loved ones, for everyone. Balance in all things.

Love
Love conquers all. Love embraces all. Love is all, the be-all and the end-all, although there is no end to love! Feel the energy of God's love with us now, supplying everything we need if only we allow ourselves to blend with it, to know it, to incorporate it. This requires another state of awareness, an expansion as well as a particular focus to become aware of the quality of energy, the quality of spirit that is available and palpable. Let's be there now, be here now, be together as one. This is the greatest need of the moment. Breathe.

Truth
Perk up your ears! Reach toward an expanded quality of listening that allows us to perceive the truth, the energy that is real, that lies beyond and within the "stuff" of daily concern. Listen for and to the truth that is, as it reveals itself in each moment. Listen and breathe.

Life
Let life prevail. Not our thoughts about life, not our aspirations about success, riches, fame or anything else! Let life, already present, already vibrant, already in motion, let life prevail. Breathe.

Purity
There is a constant, continuous flow of purification already happening beyond our efforts, beyond our wants. Let the creative process work. Our efforting mainly serves to cloud the process. It's not needed! Our intention to keep clear, pure, open to life, our commitment to the process, these do the job. Keep the ego-mind out. Keep out! Let the purification continue. Spirit knows what it's doing, it knows what to do!

Blessing
I want to bring blessing. I want to be a blessing. I also want to receive the blessings that flow in my direction! Blessings come, blessings go. Feel into the energy of blessing, lending your individual and collective energy to magnify the field, to make it available to anyone who has ears to hear and a heart to receive. And so the

ripples of blessing move out...

Single Eye
We have the capacity to see as One, to be open to the one force of love, to be focused unilaterally, yet with unlimited scope, on our immediate environment and to universes beyond.

New Earth
We seek, we trust, we trust in the ability of Spirit to enfold all, to include all, however horrendous-seeming. We need to hold steady in our faith in something greater, something truer. And when we waver from the path, to bring ourselves back, one moment at a time, one experience at a time, back into the knowing that all is well on a significant level, a level that impacts everything and moves us toward a higher state of consciousness.

Closing balance
All is well. I may feel ill, I may be experiencing pain, I may feel lonely and scared. Still, all is well. There is a constant flow, there is a greater Whole. My awareness allows me to merge with that Whole and draw strength from it, draw courage from it and keep my faith in goodness alive.

JD

Seeing connection

Lately I have been aware of what I give my attention to and how I respond to what comes to me. What do I embrace into my being? Start by being conscious of your breathing, open yourself up to the life force that we know, to the angelic beings that we are.

Opening balance
Open to the Spirit of Balance. Breathe in the Spirit of Balance and breathe out balance. Be aware of what is present in the atmosphere: with what do we come into balance? We allow the expression of the angelic being that we are to flood through our bodies, minds and hearts, and we connect with the angelic being of each other. Some people call it the spark of life (and sometimes that spark is pretty dim). We acknowledge the spark, allow it to grow and manifest into our worlds. Breathe.

Love
We let the spark of the Spirit of Love within each of us expand through our bodies, through both the physical body and the energetic body beyond the physical. We allow spirit to flood through our worlds, as we look at our worlds through the eyes of love, seeing the blessings of the rain, the flowers, the plants and fruits around us, connecting with the abundance of life in the spirit of love. Breathe.

Truth
We allow ourselves to be wisdom seekers. When we are

in the field of love, wisdom is a natural product. We bring wisdom into everything we do on a daily basis. When we speak, we speak with wisdom. We look for the truth behind all that we see and bring that awareness forward into our lives. Knowing we are creator-beings, we allow all that we create to come from the place of stillness, the place of wisdom. Breathe wisdom.

Life
We allow the life force to radiate through our being. We become conscious of what we radiate through our words, through our actions, through our thoughts. When I look at something, do I gaze with the radiance of love? When I am listening, do I hear the radiance of love? Can I discern where the love lies? Can I connect with the love? What is the nature of my attention, of my expression, of my radiation?

Radiation is an interesting word. At times we associate it with healing and at other times with danger — for example, the dangers of chemical radiation. It is undeniable that the energy pattern we emit, what radiates outward from us, has an effect. Is that effect a healing one? Is that effect a dangerous one? Or a loving one? What do I radiate into my world? Let's align with the life force coursing through us. Allow the vitality and radiance to move in, through and out. Breathe with it, radiant life in, radiant life out.

Purification
I move through my days with a sense of assurance, expressing love for the world around me, love for family,

love for friends, love for humankind, for the animal and plant world and for this planet. I live in a space of assurance that all is well because I am here. Not only am I here, but I am connected — connected to the life force, connected to angelic being, connected to what some call God. I allow myself to be connected to the Supreme Being and the manifestation of love on earth.

Blessing
We have the realization that we are connected, that we are a living expression of angelic being. We came on earth to provide a blessing. As we provide that blessing, we receive all the blessings that life has to offer and the awareness that we are the expression of a blessed life.

Single Eye
We are connected to the greater Whole. There is a tranquility that we bring, a sense of tranquility, a sense of peace, a sense of harmony. Knowing who we are, that we are the blessed one who can bring tranquility and harmony into our worlds, we let that expand outward. You know when you walk into someone's presence whether they are in harmony with themselves, and when they are, what a joy it is to be around. Breathe in harmony, breathe out tranquility.

New Earth
We have the patience to let our unique contributions be fully realized. The patience to let unfold what needs to unfold, in its own time. The patience to participate in the creative process. The wisdom to know when to step in, when to step out and when to hold steady.

When there's a new moon, people say, "There's not much going on then." Yet the energy that is present at the new moon in the point of stillness is the same energy that you feel when the moon is full, when there's a lot of activity. It is a different rate of vibration. When you work with the spirit of patience and the energy of the new moon and the stillness, then the seeds that are planted are allowed to grow. Allow yourself to be comfortable with the stillness of the energy as it moves into the creative process. Allow what needs to happen to proceed at its own pace, trusting the timing, trusting the process.

Closing balance
Bless this time, knowing all of these spirits are in balance and in harmony with each other, and are expressed within their own time and place.

JE

Body wisdom

I sit down in a quiet space, ready to attune with a higher state of consciousness. I align my body, notice my breath, deep and full. I tune into something more focused, yet more inclusive. I listen. I hear the breeze blowing through the lilac bushes outside my window, the caw-caw of a crow in the distance, the hum of a car going by. In this moment of focused attention on nothing, yet on everything in my environment, both external and internal, I am aware of a great silence, am drawn to a sensation deep in my chest, feel my shoulders drop in relaxation.

I listen. I am confident I will hear a clear voice from within, a voice I know to be mine and yet not mine, a voice that is elusive yet ever-present, a voice that is in every one of us if we make the space for it to be heard. I feel a wave of reverence pass through me, find my hands folded one over the other on my chest, my eyes gently closed, my attention focused, expectant.

Love
I listen for the words that love will bring today. Oh great Spirit of Love speak your magic, lift me up to your vibration. I am here to hear and what do I hear? Silence. Silence, followed by a deep, slow, full in-breath and a slow, measured out-breath. A sense of peace envelops my being. All is well. Love is ever present. Come to me. Come with me. Be with me. I am yours.

Truth
Oh great Spirit of Truth and Wisdom, please bring

whatever guidance you would offer and which I am ready to receive. Again, silence. I feel my body sinking into the chair. A huge yawn opens my throat and stretches my jaw... and another, and another. My hands find their way behind me on the chair, my head tilts upwards, my shoulders stretch. Another yawn. I understand that this is my body sharing its wisdom as I open myself to listen.

Life
Oh great Spirit of Life, inform my capacities from your higher plane. What is needed in the greater Whole in this energy field which is "me"? Another yawn. Another body movement, a kind of swaying. My head drops forward; my shoulders circle gently. I am aware of tension releasing, of letting go of muscular tension (and who knows what other stresses). There are no words, only these bodily directives playing out.

Purification
Dear God, please guide me as to what is most vital in this day, with this remarkable group of resonant individuals all around me?

Quiet, peace and focused attention. Taking time to LISTEN to the body's wisdom. The need for rest, the need for movement, the need to honor the organic rhythms that play out in our daily cycles. Really FOLLOWING the body's directives will enable the process of purification. And this is true on every level of being, all the capacities — mental rest, emotional clearing, spiritual availability.

Blessing
We need to participate in the blessing process. This is not something that is done to us, nor are we required to "produce" it. A proactive stance is required. This is difficult to describe. We need to be in position to align with Spirit and to catch the blessing-vibe and embody it, embrace it, become it even as it is emerging and revealing itself to us, so that it can proceed through us, with our blessing deliberately given.

Single Eye
Blessing is everywhere. All of the gifts of life, each sight, each sound, each moment. It is all perfect, it is all sacred, it is all a source of blessing and a potential vehicle for offering blessing. We have choice in every moment: to be grounded in the blessing-flow or to resist and reject it. What comes to mind is the classic Attunement teaching that designates cursing or complaint as the absence of blessing. Not the opposite, but the lack of, an absence of the spirit of blessing. For me, this is reason to pause and self-reflect.

New Earth
What emits from me? What frequency do I broadcast? What atmosphere emanates from me as I move through my moments, through my days, through my lifespan? The approach that my Attunement colleague Linda Tisch applies in her life is this: "The focus of my daily living is the quality of my spiritual expression."

This is no small undertaking and may be the Way to a better world.

Closing balance
How invigorating to be able to share in this level of consideration of what it means to be human. How challenging, yet satisfying to re-commit my lifeblood, my life force, my energy to the best of my ability and bring whatever blessing I can in this world. And it begins right here, right now. I bless this body, this mind, this heart, these connections, these relationships. The one in me, the one in you, the one in all of us.

JD

PEACE

Peace in every heart

I take a moment to ponder, what is the need of the day?

Without pause this comes: peace, peace in every heart.

Peace in one heart is a major contribution! The Dalai Lama said, reflecting on the terrorist attacks in Paris in November 2015, "We need a systemic approach to foster humanistic values of oneness and harmony." My question: what can we, as caring humans and Attunement practitioners, contribute to this systemic approach? Is Attunement itself a systemic approach? If not, how do we make it so? If so, how do we spread the word, and the practice?

Love
How do we access the greatest love possible and maintain focus there? How do we enhance, deepen, and expand our experience of love in every conscious moment? Let's breathe into these questions. Let's commune with the vibration of love.

Truth
What is the truth for me? How do I nurture both my understanding and my practice of true expression? How do I convey my understanding and embodiment of truth to others? How do I receive theirs, all the while striving to foster oneness and harmony?

Life
Let's allow the vital current of life to course through our

veins. How well are we doing at letting go of any anti-life thoughts, feelings, words or actions? Let's let go of these as we breathe in the Spirit of Life. Let's allow life-giving emotions to flow through our hearts.

How can we hone these skills? Are we honest with ourselves in facing our own shortcomings? Without acknowledging our own truths, we can't do better, we can't contribute to the systemic change toward peace. Let's face ourselves just as we are and re-avow the intention to be the change towards peace and harmony.

Purification
Let my heart be purified, let me be cleansed of self-serving attitudes and practices, however well disguised as religion, politics or self-betterment of any kind. In other words, false values that detract from, rather than contribute to, oneness. Let my heart know peace, that's all I seek and I know You listen when I speak.

Blessing
Blessings abound, do we see them? Do we receive them? Breathe blessings in, blessings out.

Single Eye
Peace, oneness, harmony. Let me focus on these qualities of vibratory substance. Knowing that each of us is committed to this uni-purpose, our contribution to the systemic upliftment of humanity is exponentially increased. Let me focus on my part in achieving this sacred goal.

New Earth
Let's be a part of bringing the New Earth into reality. We already are a part of that; let's renew and fortify our resolve. And let's live and breathe the embodiment of peace, of oneness, of harmony now, in all ways, in all our days.

Closing balance
Let's breathe together in the awareness of our sacred responsibility. May we, each one, know peace, know harmony, experience oneness as we part company on this plane, trusting that the Great Mystery will continue to weave its magic until we meet again.

JD

Sun shine on me

Sun shine on me
Warm me, warm my heart.
Let your light shine
Healing the places of dark.

Let your colors
Bring the warmth you are
Shining on me.
You're my morning star.

Let the darkness fall away from me.
You can burn it with eternity.
Let my heart know peace, that's all I seek.
And I know You listen when I speak.

Sun shine on me
Warm me, warm my heart.
Let your light shine
Healing the places of dark.

JD

Peace within, peace without

The theme for today is peace. I was thinking of the song, "Let There Be Peace on Earth." I particularly enjoy a version of the song which includes the words: "Let there be peace in me." How much peace do I really have within my internal world? How does my internal world affect my external world?

Opening balance
We open to the spirit of balance. Breathe into your point of stillness. Breathe deeply, relax as you breathe out.

Let's open ourselves to the wonderful vibration of peace, the sense of peace that passes all understanding. We allow something new to come into our experience when we are conscious of that particular vibration: old problems can't be solved at the level of vibration at which they were created. The vibration of peace is calming, relaxing. There is just as much energy available in aligning with the frequency of peace as in aligning with the energy of frantic activity. Physically, we may feel more energized. Let's breathe in peace, breathe out peace.

Love
We open to the spirit of divine love, to the heavenly vibrations. We allow peace to come through and cleanse every cell of our body, to cleanse our whole energy field. We let that sense of love and peace expand through us and into our creative field. We allow whatever is jagged in us, any incoherent energy, to find harmony within the sense of peace. We allow whatever needs to move out of our energy fields to dissipate and return to the

creative cycle. Breathe in love, breathe out peace.

Truth
We move into the pituitary, the brow area, the Spirit of Truth. We are created in harmony, the truth of ourselves is peace. We bring that into our worlds.

Life
We move to the thyroid, the throat area, the Spirit of Life. This is where the specific essences that we bring into the world throughout our lives are differentiated. The current of life moves strongly here. We live our lives with the sense of peace that we are designed to bring. We breathe peace in and breathe peace out.

Purification
We move to the heart-thymus area, which focuses the Spirit of Purification. What is in the heavens of ourselves is pure and as we allow that vibrational quality to move through us, all of the distortions that are in the earth can be affected by our sense of peace. As we allow the light to come into our expression, it dispels the darkness, the distortions.

The heart can sense things far quicker than the mind and it takes a few nanoseconds to respond to stimuli that come to us. We can use that brief gap in time to choose to respond with a sense of peace, a sense of the divine. We breathe through the heart, allowing that which is pure and holy to be expressed through our hearts. We bring the breath of life into the world, our breath of life. We share that breath and atmosphere with all. We are connected with all through our breathing.

Blessing
We move to the pancreas area, the Spirit of Blessing. We bring into our world an awareness of the abundance, of the giving and receiving of blessings. Do we look for the blessing in each of our waking moments? It can be a full-time job! As things are presented to us, do we see the blessing? Do we see ourselves as part of that blessing?

Single Eye
We move to the adrenals, the Spirit of the Single Eye. We are all one, we are all connected in the place of peace. And each of us has a particular purpose, a gift that is coming to focus within ourselves, something unique to bring into the Whole so that the spirit of God can be known on earth. There is need for the diversity among us. Looking at the various locations we represent, we see each location with its diversity and uniqueness, and yet know it's all part of the whole. Can we see ourselves as part of that whole and each bring our share of peace in our own unique way?

New Earth
We move to the reproductive glands, the gonads, the Spirit of the New Earth. This is how our world is created: we let peace descend from the higher realms into our being and out through us. We extend that sense of peace as we connect with our personal worlds, bringing peace into our daily living, through thought, word and action. This is where our internal world becomes evident in our everyday living.

Closing balance

We return to the spirit of balance, allowing Spirit to find a new balance, a new harmonic, which penetrates and strengthens our energy fields. We move forward with a sense of peace, of new possibility. Breathe into the sense of peace, into the new balance, into the new possibilities that have been opened up. No matter the season and level of activity, we welcome in the new and let go of the old. We do that in peace. We can do that consciously in peace.

JE

Serenity

Today is Mother's Day and I was thinking about mothers and how we appreciate them. The term "Mother God" also came to me. I don't know how to describe either Mother God or Father God: what I do know is that we are angelic beings here on Earth. We need to spend more time looking within for answers, instead of looking beyond ourselves. One of the words that keeps coming to me is serenity, tranquil serenity.

Opening balance
Let's breathe and come into balance within ourselves. As we do, we feel a sense of serenity, the calmness of our being, all the chaos around us simply drifts away. There's a knowing that we are together across the miles and that we are loved.

Love
Love is the life force that creates all, that is the reality of who we are. We don't have to go searching for it, we just are. We allow the life force of love to flow through us and into our worlds.

Truth
When we allow love to flow through us, we touch into the wisdom within, the wisdom of knowing who we are, knowing we are in the right place at the right time. We breathe in the love that we are and breathe out the wisdom that we are. Wisdom is beyond knowledge. Wisdom is the awareness that we are creator-beings and knowing that, we radiate love and wisdom into our

worlds.

Life
I become conscious of my thoughts, my thoughts lead to words, my words lead to action and that is what radiates into my world. I become aware of the effects of my presence when I walk into a room. Do I bring chaos? Confusion? Or do I bring joy, happiness and serenity? The serenity that comes with knowing all is well, that I'm in the presence of other creator-beings and that all is well?

Purification
Do I bring assurance into my world, secure in the awareness that our connection is with Source itself? Do I have the confidence to believe in the truth of myself, in the truth of you, the assurance of knowing why we are gathered together, what we touch into in Life? The assurance that all is well, that whatever we are bringing is the right thing to bring: our talents, our essences, the uniqueness of who we are.

Blessing
These are the blessings we offer. Our awareness and our openness to spirit. The realization that we have a profound desire to invite others into the awareness, into the radiance, to share our blessings.

Single Eye
When we feel the assurance, the serenity, the tranquility of being at ease with ourselves, it allows that inner peace to be outwardly known. The mind relaxes, it

knows serenity, it no longer needs to find a reason to be. It rests in the knowing that I am open to life, open to love, open to letting that flow.

New Earth
With assurance comes patience, the patience to live in the now, the patience to accept what is. When I accept what is, I can see the beauty that is around me, I can accept without being attached.

When I have the patience to accept being in the now, being in the flow, I can let the past drift wherever it needs to go. I can take the steps I need to take, knowing what needs to stay with me and what needs to be let go of. When I accept the now, I can see options, I can see directions, I can let life unfold, and see my part in it. And I can be at peace with whatever is.

Closing balance
I can be at peace, knowing who I am: a being created in love. I see the God within you and greet the God within you from the God within me. With that, comes a knowing that we are in balance, the internal world and the external world are in harmony with each other and there are blessings in all things.

JE

SEEING CLEARLY

Freedom from attachment

I've noticed that various attachments, ranging from obvious to insidious, are holding me back these days, are pulling me down, like glue that has gone stale, but still manages to stick! Where there is attachment, there cannot be freedom. I've found it useful to examine assumptions, even searching out assumptions I didn't know I had, and putting them under a magnifying glass.

Love
Open, open way up. Open to the Way, open to the Tao. Let the Spirit of Love pour in through the crown of your head. There is so much love, so much love ready and willing to come in. Let it come. Breathe it into your system. Feel the love. Feel the love. Feel the love. You are loved. Feel the love vibration in you. Feel it moving, flowing, finding its rightful place, everywhere. Love is in you. Love is all around, love is all there is and love is in you, with you. Love IS you. You are love. You are one with love. Love is one with you. There is no separation. It's one big, juicy sea of love.

Truth
Open to the truth, open way up, open to the way of truth. Truth is not an abstract, out-there reality, but rather what appears in each moment right before your eyes, directly in your path, in your hand, in your heart. Each moment, each cycle, brings its own unique requirement, its own directive. Breathe and see, listen and know. Act and notice what follows in the very next immediate moment. What draws your attention? Be true

to the moment. Be true to yourself.

Life
Open to life, feel the pulse, feel the rhythm, feel the flow. Breathe deeply in and out, in and out, letting the thrust of the life force move in the precise ways it must. Trust! Open. Allow. Breathe. Feel. Live!

Purification
Allow any attachments that may be binding you to clear out, both known attachments and attachments of which you may be unaware. Let them move right out of your energy field. Exhale as you let them go. Ask that you become more aware of the distractions that are holding you to old patterns, old behaviors, old concepts, old beliefs, old ways of doing things, old relationships that do not serve. Even old aches and pains!

Get a fresh perspective! Let the Spirit of Purification wash away and cleanse any energies that bind or hold, that cause stagnation in the flow. Breathe slowly and deeply as you perceive that it is time for these energies to go. Give them permission to leave! Allow your pure state of being and energetic potential to predominate in the field of your awareness. Know that the clearing and cleansing are in process. Breathe with grace and ease.

Blessing
Let the blessings flow! Feel the quality of energy that is present as you acknowledge and welcome these blessings. If there is a hint in your mind that this is selfish, we can give a collective chuckle and let go of

that untrue thought pattern (how well we have been brain-washed!). Feel the blessing energy. Even as you do, the energy flows through you to places and people and life forms beyond your imagining. Let the blessings flow!

Single Eye
Let the Spirit of the Single Eye shine upon you. Shine through you. Shine from you, within you, around you. There is only this moment! You needn't be pressured, confused, scattered or overwhelmed. Just relax your muscles, relax your jaw, relax your thinking brain and be present with whatever is transpiring in your immediate experience. Breathe. Feel. See. Listen. Be still. Know.

New Earth
And so the New Earth manifests! Allowing these qualities of spirit to be present — love, truth, life, purification, blessing, focus — brings forth whatever is accurate for your highest good and your highest calling in the moment.

It's no big deal. It's just what is! Breathe this Reality, unlike the reality (small r) that the world wants us to believe is ours! There is a whole other level of existence. Let's live it!

JD

Natural rhythms

As I begin the meditation, I ask of Spirit: what are we doing here? What is needed of us? What balance are we to bring? Here is what comes in response: attention to positivity — to yesness! — to hope, to openness, to trust in love, to trust that love IS the force that propels the earth and the earth of our bodies. We're here to embody this knowing, this trust in the universal Whole.

Love
We cannot stress this enough: love IS the answer. It is also the question, the context, the focus. In short, the Everything. Love conquers all. Love is all.

Truth
The truth is: what is. It is not heavy, significant or elusive. It is simply what is. Open to the moment, bring the mind into alignment with Spirit and the truth miraculously appears every time. Every moment. In every situation. This Sanskrit quote comes to mind: "When the spirit is clear, free of all worry, truth will appear in a state of absolute nakedness." Our job is to tame the mind, one person at a time, one mind at a time, focusing on one's own mind.

Life
Look around. Look at the function of nature. Nature presents (itself). Nature allows. Nature moves with the seasons, with the natural rhythms that surround and inform it. The tree doesn't attempt to control its fate. The leaf doesn't aspire to be on the other tree or even to

be in a different place on its own tree. There is full acceptance, an embracing of the reality in which it finds itself. Life, then, has no resistance in nature. Ponder how this measures up with human resistance. Let's take a lesson from nature.

Purification
Let not your heart be troubled. Let life move through unimpeded. Let the purification process be ever-present and continuous. As multiple stimuli bombard the system, let the energy of purification penetrate the chaotic activity, no matter how impossible circumstances appear to be. Be at peace.

Blessing
Can I be a blessing, no matter what? No matter what my current circumstances are? No matter the state of my health, finances, relationships, working life? Look around. Look at the offerings, the contributions to your existence. Is anything lacking? Is anything wrong? Does anything need to be different? Bless my world and everything in it. Everything. Every thing. Every one. Even myself!

Single Eye
Let's keep a single focus: one moment at a time. One source from which to view the world, the divine source. See through those eyes and there is only one sight to be seen in each moment. It's not difficult, confusing, overwhelming or terrifying. Just keep moving, one step at a time, opening your eyes and seeing what is there, what is here. Notice your thoughts, but don't let them

direct your action. Keep focused in Source, ask: what would Love have me do?

New Earth
Following along this path of discovery, we evolve our perceptions, actions and experiences as we keep focused in Spirit. Then individually and collectively we spiral upwards, however slowly, however imperceptibly, but inexorably, onward and upward!

Closing balance
Our sacred responsibility is for each of us, right where we are, right here, right now (in every moment) to see with open eyes, with alignment of heart and mind focused in Spirit.

JD

Sanctification
by Louise Broomberg

Evening wraps around me
like an old familiar shawl,
warm and comforting.
I snuggle in,
this day's journey complete.
What rose petals have I strewn
on the path I trod today?
How many times did I see
the face of the Beloved?
Did I look into the eyes of Love
and see my own Self
shining back at me?

Joy, appreciation, self-love

It is often said that if you do not love and appreciate yourself, it is difficult to truly love and appreciate another. How often do we deflect appreciation directed towards ourselves? When was the last time you said to yourself, "job well done"? This meditation reminds us of who or what we really are. When we don't love ourselves, we are incomplete: self-love calls us to be Whole. I have used the pronoun "I" as this is a meditation on self-love. Enjoy.

I take three breaths. I allow my mind to come to rest. I feel my body relax. I breathe into wholeness, allowing the vibration of appreciation to flow through my whole body, allowing the vibration of self-appreciation to flow through my body temple. I see myself as a radiant being, full of compassion, kindness, beauty, love and light.

This is the truth of myself. I acknowledge the opportunities to express self-love in my everyday experiences. I practice compassion. When doubt or self judgement arises, I breathe. I let self-doubt move into a neutral place and pass on. Breathe.

In wisdom, I practice self-love. I express my creative being in all that I do. I smile inwardly. I take myself lightly. I see myself in the light of the truth of who I really am, as a creator being.

The more I care for myself, the more I express

compassion, caring, acceptance, peace. The more my world will respond in kind.

I appreciate all that I am: the good, the challenges, the indifferences, the beauty. It is all one.

I acknowledge the blessings in my life. They encourage me to be thankful in all things, to see the good around me, to accept challenges, to grow.

I live in a multifaceted world, a complex world where there is a need for both thankfulness and forgiveness. I need to forgive myself for withholding love from areas of my life that bring me pain, that bring me grief, despair, anger. I consciously love myself during these times of discomfort, and as I do, it becomes easier to absorb and transmute these feelings to neutral energy.

As I trust in my own divine nature, my presence invites others to know their own truth and to begin to experience self-love.

I breathe in the fullness of my world and all its possibilities, the adventures, the quiet times, the peace and I breathe in the fulfillment that love brings.

JE

Remembering our creativity

During the opening discussion on our monthly teleconference, there was a lot of energy around the theme of creativity. As we move into the meditation, be conscious of how creativity is in every aspect of our lives and is expressed differently through each of us, depending on life circumstances and where we are in the cycle of life.

Opening balance
Breathe. Be conscious of your breath, the rhythm of your breathing.
Open yourself to the Divine, to Source and allow the creative spirit of life to flow through you and nourish you, to bathe you in the sweet essences of life.

Love
We allow the creative Spirit of Love that we are to fully surround our bodies and nourish every cell. As we connect with the love that's within each of us, we look at our worlds through the eyes of love and recognize why we are here: to bring the Spirit of Love into action on earth.

Truth
We allow the wisdom that is already in us to guide our actions, trusting that whatever we need to know will come to us, if we are willing to open ourselves to the Spirit of Love. We maintain the connection with Source. We discern where we need to be, what we need to do. We accept the truth of who we are: precious angelic beings. In wisdom, we let judgement pass away.
Breathe.

Life
Recognizing that life is precious, that all lives, even our own, are created in love, in wisdom, in truth, we value each moment of our living. We breathe in the life essence and with each out-breath, we release love and wisdom into our worlds.

We are creator-beings and each one of us has a specific part to play. We welcome the talents of others, knowing that we work together in the spirit of cooperation, knowing that all of our talents and all of our creative gifts are needed. We breathe that breath of life.

Purification
Let our hearts be pure. Let our hearts be connected. We allow whatever is in the heavens of our being to come into the earth in a clear and loving way. We allow whatever is in the earth to be refined in that love, so we can truly say, "as above, so below." Breathe.

Blessing
We give great thanks for being together, each in our specific location, and for the strength of the connections between us in the Spirit of Love. Being together allows more creativity to come into our worlds, generates more potential for creative action.

The ability to receive the blessings of life is a big step towards accepting ourselves. We don't need to make apologies for the blessings in our lives. We can receive the blessings that are coming our way, we can welcome all the bounty that the heavens and earth provide. Each of us is a blessing and collectively the blessing-energy that emanates from us is magnified. Breathe out this frequency of blessing and extend that opportunity to others.

Single Eye
We know the oneness; we are at one with Spirit. This allows each of us to bring into the world what we need to bring, allows the Spirit of Love to come into the world in a very fine way through each of us and that contributes to the whole.

New Earth
We bring love, wisdom and creativity into the moments of our living, into each cycle of activity. The process allows us to ground ourselves, so that the spirit of angelic being can be known in our experience, not merely in imagination. We are creator-beings throughout our lifetime. We can dispel the myth that if you haven't done it by forty, you're not going to! Possibilities are infinite, creative potential is limitless at every phase of the life cycle.

Closing balance
Breathe and relax into your day.

JE

Trust in the flow (we're all in it together)

I have been struck by a thought I heard expressed recently, that "the opposite of pain is flow." I experience that as a powerful statement and have found it to be true as I encounter different conditions and situations in myself and others. We can use this as an entry point for consideration. All that you bring, silently or spoken, is welcome and is included in our time of attunement.

Opening balance
I ponder the question: what is important for us to know and experience through this time together? What is needed for overall balance and potential for flow?

The answer that comes is unexpected, although perhaps not surprising: love.

As love flows in and out, it also passes through. As it flows in, all of the refined, pure potential energy enters our bodies, enters our fields, infuses us with life force, renews our vitality. As love flows through our bodies, every vibration in every cell resonates at a higher frequency. As we breathe out, and love flows or radiates out from our being, we gift everything and everyone in our midst with the flow of love. And so it goes. So simple and yet, so difficult to maintain, to sustain, to remember. Let's remember.

Spirit of Love
This is it! Everything is here-contained. Compassion, caring, letting go, releasing what needs to move on... the

essence of flow. Big love. Love with a capital L. The love that makes the world go around. The ultimate raw material out of which everything, known and unknown, is born. Breathe in love. Know love. Keep the "love inquiry" active and ongoing. Keep looking. Keep listening. Keep asking.

Spirit of Truth
Many so-called problems in the world come from the misconception that truth is solid. "My truth is better than your truth." "My truth will never change." It is a paradox that truth is both absolute and transitory. What is true in this moment is only true in this moment. It may be true in the next moment, but that is irrelevant in this moment. And yet, the truth in this moment is absolute. It is true and nothing else is true. The moments flow, like frames in a film, discreet, yet joined together in the flow. Moving pictures. Moving moments of truth.

Spirit of Life
Nature has the potential to teach us so much. The flow of the seasons is awesome. In the spring, bare trees begin to show minute signs of life, barely decipherable, but then, seemingly within hours, buds appear, then leaves, and a profusion of joyous green covers the trees and fields and streets. When things look bleak, do I trust in the flow? When I have a moment of sorrow or anger, do I remember that all emotions last a mere 90 seconds if I allow myself to experience fully what is here to be felt and allow the feeling to pass naturally? Trust in the flow.

Spirit of Purification
Let's purify. Let's simplify. Let's let love and truth and life be present in us, in me. It's the holding, it seems, that blocks the flow and creates dis-ease and pain. Can I breathe through the hard parts and let them soften and move gently on through?

Spirit of Blessing
Bless you. Bless me. Bless each one with all of our burdens, all of our doubts, all of our foibles. We are each doing the best we can. Another paradox! We are already living to our highest potential AND we can aim higher and higher, letting our consciousness be lifted and lifted. Forgiveness helps the flow.

Spirit of the Single Eye
One single focus, yet we have two eyes to accomplish the task. There has to be a flow between the two eyes in order to see one thing, since the eyes actually have two different perspectives. Just as I (one of me) need you (two of us) to see clearly, to be in the flow. Otherwise life is painful and distorted, since it requires two to focus. So we need each other, just as one eye needs the other, to see clearly in each moment and keep moving forward, one step at a time.

Spirit of the New Earth
In each moment, I am in a new reality, the New Earth of the moment. I AM a new reality. What is my experience? It depends on you! We are not separate entities,

contrary to appearances, but all in this (world) together. There is a unified flow that may be invisible, but is very present. This is unified radiation, isn't it? Not something we strive for, but the reality of our days on earth! We are all in the river of life, flowing in a particular direction. It takes all of us to discern where that is. Thank you for being in my flow.

JD

BODY FIELD

Chain of pearls

A friend of mine described the endocrine system as a chain of pearls. That magical phrase helped me realize what a blessing this physical form is! Without our bodies, we wouldn't be able to bring the essences of the seven spirits into practical manifestation. Our physical bodies are a vital part of the Whole and we need to give them the care and attention they deserve and we need to appreciate them!

Breathe deeply.

Spirit of Balance
Start with the Spirit of Balance, which allows the body to come into alignment. Breathe and allow the Spirit of Balance to move in, through and out. Breathe it in, breathe it out.

Spirit of Love
The Spirit of Love comes through the pineal gland, the first opening of the chain of pearls, as pure, undifferentiated life force. Love is the all-encompassing energy of divine being that enfolds us at the most refined and subtle levels. It's the spirit of God that is differentiated through us and is expressed through all aspects of our living. Breathe in the Spirit of Love, breathe out the Spirit of Love, recognizing that the energy of pure love is who we are.

Spirit of Truth
The Spirit of Truth is the first differentiation of the Spirit

of Love. This is the place within the hypothalamus, where the Spirits of Love and Truth come together and create the reality of peace, the tranquility that we feel, which allows wisdom to come into our living. We can only bring peace into the world around us when we are at peace. It is within stillness that we see our worlds clearly and are able to extend peace outwards from the truth of who we are. Breathe in from this place of stillness, breathe out.

Spirit of Life
The Spirit of Life enters the physical plane through the thyroid gland. When we know the spirits of love and truth, it gives definition to our lives. We can look at the Spirit of Life as carrying the essences of our DNA, the essences of our true nature that are primed and ready to come into form as we allow them to do so.

The thyroid controls our growth patterns and metabolic rate. It's prone to imbalance, as is evidenced by the numbers of people having overly low or high thyroid activity. Enfold all of that, maintaining a balance within your life, a balance of activity and rest. Allow love and truth to come into union, informing the Spirit of Life. Breathe.

Spirit of Purification
We move to the thymus gland, which lies next to the heart. You may have seen people tap their chest, perhaps unconsciously trying to activate the Spirit of Purification.

The thymus is the middle gland of the seven endocrines, the crossover point between the finer and denser vibratory realms (of heaven and earth). As our hearts open and become clear, what we know of Spirit can be allowed to flow through our energy fields unimpeded, to be made manifest in the earth, in form, right here at the point of now.

How open am I to let the Spirits of Love, Truth and Life come into my living? How do I perceive my world? Do I let myself get caught up in all the distortions and distractions around me or do I allow what is in the heavens to be made manifest on earth?

Spirit of Blessing
We move into the denser frequencies of the earth via the Islets of Langerhans in the pancreas. The quality of spirit that enters here is one of blessing, allowing an experience of the sweetness of life to be brought into the physical realm.

Be thankful that we not only bring the Spirit of Blessing but we also receive blessings. Look around, we are so blessed. Beauty and abundance everywhere: the sun, trees, birds, our pets and companions... and each other! Take this opportunity to bless it all and not be afraid to receive the blessings of this world and allow those blessings to ascend. Breathe.

Spirit of the Single Eye
The Spirit of the Single Eye comes through the adrenal glands. I've always looked at the Spirit of the Single Eye

as: where do I put my focus? What do I bring into focus in my world? I have a sacred responsibility to bring my unique contribution, my expression of the Spirit of Love and the Spirit of Life into the earth.

As we become more aware that we are a part of something larger than ourselves, we recognize a greater purpose, a divine purpose. We only become aware of that purpose when we consciously allow our attention to the Spirit of Love to move through us.

Spirit of the New Earth
The Spirit of the New Earth contains all the seven spirits that we have previously considered. This is what we bring into our living: the undifferentiated energy of the Spirits of Love and Truth, the Spirits of Life and Purification, and Blessing and the Single Eye. This is what we bring into our new earth in each moment.

We are creator-beings, conscious that we are co-creating our future on this earth together and without the physical form, we wouldn't be able to bring all of this into the earth at this time. What a blessing this physical form is! It is all part of the whole, the vehicle to bring God into action on earth through our living.

Closing balance
Bless our entire collective energy field and return to the Spirit of Balance, aware of who you are and what you bring into your life.

Prayer

We thank thee, Holy One, for being with us in our diverse places. We bless the technology, the physical form that assists us to be together in this way and we bless the spiritual reality that allows us to be together beyond any technology. We give great thanks for this opportunity, we bless each one in our worlds and we receive the blessings that come to us. Amen.

JE

Rainbow meditation

Listening to the news, I become aware of my own reactions and how they affect my energy field. I ask the question: how do I let these external events affect me and am I even aware that they do? This meditation invites you to become more aware of your own energy field and what you choose to allow in.

Breathe. Become aware of your breath and breathe. Place your hands about 2-4 inches from your body and gently scan your body. This is your energy.
Breathe.

Now hold your hands about 6 inches from the sides of your body. Breathe and feel that pulse. You are so much more than your physical body. You are surrounded by an energy field; some call it your aura or etheric body. We feel not only our own energy, but those energy fields around us as well: plants, pets, people, weather. We live in a communal energy field. We can pick up feelings of joy, unease, calm and more from those around us.

There are times when I ask myself: why am I feeling this way? Is this generated by me or am I picking it up from someone or somewhere else? Sometimes the feeling leaves and sometimes it stays. When I know where it is coming from, I can see what needs to be done.
Breathe.

Consciously align with Source. Let love radiate without concern for results. Let the light energy of love totally

surround you and your whole auric field.
Breathe.

Envision the golden light of love totally surrounding you and your energy field. Feel the light current as it moves to enfold you.
Breathe.

Allow the indigo light to surround you. Move your hands around your body as if scanning yourself and envision the indigo light of truth surrounding you.
Breathe.

Envision the blue light of life surrounding you, the radiance of who you are.
Breathe.

Welcome the green light energy as it surrounds you. Green represents the heart energy, the translucent pure green energy of the heart.
Breathe.

Allow the golden light of yellow to surround you.
Breathe joy.

Envision the orange light of the sunset surrounding your body. Let it flow through and fill your energy field.
Breathe, bless, joy, breathe.

Envision the red light surrounding your body. The red light grounds us. Breathe, feel the earth.
Breathe.

The light energy is all colors of the rainbow and when combined, becomes the clear white light.
Breathe in all that you are, the clear white light.
Breathe.

You are a rainbow in all its magnificence.

JE

Re-sourcing

Align. Breathe. Balance. Listen to the silence, to the stillness. Few words come. There is a sense of the body weight sinking into the chair, into the earth. A feeling of connecting, of grounding.

At this point, the energy did not wish to go to the pineal gland and the endocrine system, as in the classical Attunement schema, but rather to the root chakra, and past that, deep into the Earth. This became a chakra-based attunement meditation.

Earth chakra
Feel your deep connection with the Earth. Allow your awareness to go far down and connect. Let go of all the excess tension you carry through your body, mind and emotions. Mother Earth can and will receive it all, effortlessly and graciously. Breathe. Feel the returning pulsation of energy come upwards from deep in the earth, bringing nourishment to all levels of your energy field, to all levels of your being.

Root chakra
Breathe in the energy, up through the feet, up through the bottom of the torso, up through the midline of the body and let it disperse into your body-field. Feel the richness of the mother energy, bringing nutrients from the earth into your body, bringing health, bringing wholeness. Breathe.

Sacral/navel area
There is one energetic vortex in front of the navel area and one in back of the sacrum. Breathe in the energy of birth and creativity. Breathe it in and let it go where it may.

Solar plexus
In this area resides your internal sun, both front and back, the center of your personal power, your "I can." Feel your personal sun smiling, a sweet, pure, innocent, smile — the essence of you. Breathe it in, let it be. Let yourself be, just the way you are.

Heart chakra (again, front and back are included)
Feel into the center of love and compassion, including self-love and self-compassion. Feel into your capacity to forgive others and to forgive yourself. Breathe in the capacity to love, forgive and have compassion. Breathe into this center, this resource, this wellspring of creative energy.

Throat chakra
Here is the center of our will to overcome difficulty, to take action — right action. Have faith in your own radiance, however that translates into your unique expression. Breathe in life force, breathe out what needs to be emitted.

Brow chakra
Feel into the center of your natural knowing, intuition, vision. Trust that constant source of wisdom, coming from your higher self. We tap into something vast and

unchanging, eternal, yet accessible in the moment. Let's use this resource to re-source, to inform and support our day-to-day thought, word and action.

Crown chakra
Continuing the upward movement, the energy vortex moves to the top of the head, completing a spiral of energy from earth to crown. As the energy continues upwards, we return our thanks to the Creator, to Sacred Unity, to Spirit, the vibrational reality that fuels everything. The flow of energy that comes up through the crown, spills over like a fountain into our upraised palms and fills all of our capacities.

Closing balance
Let the energy that has moved through our energy fields integrate and balance. Let it distribute harmoniously. Let it propel us forward into the NOW. Amen: May our future actions grow from here.*

JD

This meaning of "amen" is taken from a translation of the Aramaic Lord's Prayer that influenced this meditation and which can be found on the following page.

The Aramaic Lord's Prayer
(Douglas-Klotz translation)

The original language spoken by Jesus was Aramaic. The Aramaic language is so constructed that one word can have many meanings. According to Aramaic speaker and scholar Neil Douglas-Klotz, here is how the prayer might read if translated directly from the Aramaic.

O Breathing Life, your name shines everywhere!
Release a space to plant your Presence here.
Envision your "I can" now.
Embody your desire in every light and form.
Grow through us this moment's bread and wisdom.
Untie the knots of failure binding us, as we release the strands we hold of others' faults.
Help us not forget our Source, yet free us from not being in the Present.
From you arises every vision, power and song, from gathering to gathering.
Amen: may our future actions grow from here!

Field of flowers, field of love

We are in the wake of the Solstice and Christmas is just around the corner. This is a sacred time, a turning point, regardless of one's hemisphere, particular perspective or level of activity. The minute pause at the point of turning marks the precise moment the energy floods in. Where is my attention turned, to what am I attuning as the pause occurs before the directional shift?

My heart is full to overflowing during these special days. I am finding that tears spring to my eyes at the slightest nudge from my surroundings: someone's suffering, a beautiful musical phrase, a fleeting thought, almost anything can trigger the wave of emotion. I am paying attention, to discern what is inside the emotion.

As I tune in to this moment, words and phrases come to awareness: field of love, field of flowers, hearts as one, feel each other. Decency, respect, compassion, peace. Namaste. From my center to yours, we are one.

Opening balance

What is needed?
Quiet. Slow down.
Breathe.
Sit.
Elongate the spine.
Let the energy flow.

These words come:*
My energy channels are open, open... open!
My energy blockages are going, going... gone!
I am completely healed.
My body is healed.
My mind is healed.
My heart is healed.

Love
Love heals all wounds, whatever the form, whatever and whenever the source. Breathe in the healing balm of love, the highest, purest vibratory substance available. Feel it enter and permeate the field: your body-field, my body-field, our body-field. Let's imagine we are healing the field of every person on earth. We are alive in a field of love and it is everywhere.

Truth
In this field, I am aware only of what is true for me now, my attention naturally goes where the energy needs to flow. As each of us allows our mind to attend to what is needed, a rhythmic pattern — a pulsation — reveals itself and may even be discernible as thought. Let's listen.

Life
Why would I want to fight or resist the life force? Why would you? Let's get with it! Let's get on with it! Let's allow, even encourage, the current of life to course through our veins. Let's welcome the power, the movement, the constant change of intensity and revel in the ALIVENESS of it all.

Purity
Let the spirit of purity envelop and imbue my energy field so that nothing distorts the higher, finer vibratory pattern. Let my mind be clear and my heart be as pure as my consciousness allows. Let me be a space where love and truth may flourish.

Blessing
A song snippet comes to mind, a memory from singing hymns at school: "Praise God from whom all blessings flow." Praise. Be grateful. Raise your voice on high. Raise your eyes, look upward. Come away with me to greener pastures where the blessings truly flow, where the peaceful waters flow. Bless and be blessed, in no particular order, be blessed and bless works equally well. B-less. Be less self-conscious, less busy, less critical, less vain. B-less and bless. It's an example of less is more! Be more effective in bringing peace to the world. Bless and praise and bless some more.

Single Eye
Let your focus be clear. Get centered. Plant your feet on the ground and listen to Spirit. What would love have me do now? Take time, slow down. Let's breathe slowly and deeply together, natural rhythms will find their way through us. Do you feel the beat? Do you see the uni-focus? Are you present in your body? All capacities come together as one — in you, in me — and together we are one.

New Earth
And so we create the New Earth. May hope and peace prevail.

JD

From the practice of Chunyi Lin, Spring Forest Qigong

GROUNDING

Still meadow trees

This meditation took place while I was attending an Attunement gathering at Still Meadow Retreat Center in Oregon in December of 2014.

Spirit of Balance
Let's breathe easy. Mmm (sigh). Imagine being surrounded by the white light of love. This morning, there was a gorgeous, vibrant, pink sunrise. Let the beauty of that vibrant pink sunrise enfold you. If you can, look out your window into the vastness of nature, know we are all one even though we're not in the same room together.
Allow the energy to come into balance and breathe.

Pineal
Be open to the life force of all as it comes through the crown, into the pineal gland and envelops the body. As I look out my window and see the magnificent trees, my eye is drawn to one evergreen. I see the vastness of this tree and know that we are connected. The pinecones remind me of the pineal gland, which has a similar shape. Breathe in the spirit of connection, the Spirit of Love.
Breathe.

Pituitary
We allow the oneness of Spirit to come down through us into the pituitary: it allows us to see beyond the physical, and to know that we are connected. And in that connection to each other, we're connected to

everything in this world, connected to the beauty of it.
Breathe.

When the pineal and pituitary are balanced together, there's another rhythm that is created, that is inviolate. Feel that rhythm, feel the connection.
Breathe.

Thyroid
We move into the thyroid, feel the life force, the essences of life! If something is blocked in the throat area it affects your ability to communicate, whether it's your voice or your intention. Allow the radiance of who you are to move into your world. Each one of our essences is needed to make this world complete.
Breathe.

Thymus
We move into the thymus, the Spirit of Purification, the crossover point between heaven and earth. Allow what needs to come from our heavenly experience into the earth, allow our earthly nature to rise up into the heavens so that what needs to arise can, what needs to stay may and what needs to return to the creative cycle may.
Breathe.

Skeletal system
Place one hand on the outside of each shoulder and enter the long bone or skeletal system. Our bones ground us into the earth. I am looking out my window and all the trees have lost their leaves. I can see the

structure of the tree and how it grows from the roots. The branches are bare and look very similar to the roots. I can see the outline of the tree's "skeletal system." We also have skeletal systems; we can only imagine what they look like. Visualize the torso as your trunk.

Shoulders
Imagine a line running from shoulder to shoulder and your two hands enfolding the shoulders.
Breathe. Hold the pattern for a few seconds.

Envision a line from one shoulder to the opposite hip and one of your hands radiating to each.
Breathe, hold until you feel the energy shift.

Now switch to the other shoulder and hip. Breathe. When you do that, you cross over and cover the whole trunk of your body.
Breathe. Let the energy balance.
Breathe.

Hips
Envision your hands enfolding both hips and breathe. Here, you are touching into the whole pelvic area.
Breathe, hold, bless.

Keep one hand on one hip and move the other hand to the opposite foot: this will really ground you!
Breathe.

Switch hands to the other hip and foot, hold.

Breathe.

Feet
Then, with your two hands, enfold your two feet. Our feet touch the earth more than any other part of the body.
Bless them, feel that connection with the earth.
Breathe.

Shoulders
Move back to the shoulders.
Breathe, hold, balance.

Jaw
Envision one hand radiating to a shoulder and the other hand to the opposite side of the jaw.
Breathe, hold.

We rarely consider the jaw and all the work it does, yet, we often hold tension in the jaw and neck area.
Breathe, hold.

Switch hands and sides.
Breathe, hold.

Radiate to both sides of the jaw.
Breathe, hold.

Closing balance
Return to the shoulders and notice how the energy has shifted.
Breathe.

Take both hands, sweep over your head and gently down to your feet.

Just breathe together and let the energy come to a beautiful rest as we begin a new day.

JE

Hand attunement

We will do something a little different today. I am going to direct you in a meditation involving your hands. This can be useful in sharing energy with ourselves or with others at a distance.

Opening balance
To begin, hold your hands a comfortable distance apart. Feel the energy and we'll start with the spirit of balance.

Breathe.

Temples
We will go to the temples with open hands to bless our head and brain. Keep your hands a few inches from your head until you feel a gentle, even pulse between the hands.

Breathe.

Eyes
Move to the eyes with the flat of the hands, or one hand in front of the eyes and one hand behind the head at eye level. The eyes have contact points that touch into all parts of the body and this can be extremely relaxing. When you are in a life cycle of high energy and things appear chaotic, this can calm the mind and body.

Breathe.

Hands
Use your right hand (R) to direct the energy and the left hand (L) to receive. The hands, as the eyes, have contact points that touch into the rest of the body. The seven spirits are also represented on the hand.

Spirit of Love
Point your R index finger to the top of the L thumb to access the pineal gland. Breathe in the Spirit of Love, let the energy of the Spirit of Love flow through your body.

Breathe, hold, bless.

Spirit of Truth
Move to the Spirit of Truth, the pituitary gland. The R thumb is placed in front of the L thumbnail and the R index finger is behind. Breathe in wisdom. Breathe out the truth of who you are, let it radiate into your world.

Breathe.

Spirit of Life
The Spirit of Life, the thyroid gland, is located on the outside of the L thumb where it reaches the hand. Place your R thumb and index finger on either side of the thumb at the base. Breathe in the spirit of life, the union of love and truth, the divine pattern before it comes into the earth.

Breathe.

Spirit of Purification

Focus on the heart contact point, just below the L ring finger. The thymus is located right next to the heart. Direct the energy through the R index finger toward the heart/thymus point. Feel the energy field, allow the angelic spirit of purification, of clarity, to symbolically move into your earthly form.

Breathe.

Spirit of Blessing
The Spirit of Blessing, the pancreas. The contact point is the area between the L thumb and the first finger. Direct the energy through the R index finger. Be conscious of our blessings, receive the blessing, be the blessing, extend the blessing.

Breathe.

Spirit of the Single Eye
The Spirit of the Single Eye, the adrenals. The point of contact is just into the fleshy part below the L thumb. Direct the energy with your R hand into the adrenal point. The adrenals have a dual purpose: what do we focus on? Fight or flight? Love and tranquility? The Single Eye symbolizes that we are all a part of the Whole, the One. We're in this earth together with every living thing and being.

Breathe.

Spirit of the New Earth
The Spirit of the New Earth, the reproductive glands.

The contact point is the middle of the inside of the L wrist. Direct the energy with your R hand into the contact point. What do we bring forth in our living? In our world? Do we bring creativity, peace, newness?

Breathe.

Closing balance
Hold your world between your hands. As the energy balances, bless your hands and all they do, bless your world, bless the opportunity to share in this experience. Breathe.

JE

Feet on the ground

When we meditate, we are at one with ourselves and spirit. We allow something new to come into our awareness. It may be a feeling, looking at something familiar in a new way or from a different perspective, or it may be a whole new idea or direction. We will begin with the first four spirits and then move to the skeletal system to ground ourselves.

Opening balance
Take a deep breath and as you open to the Spirit of Balance, read this poem by Diana Durham called "New Bearings."

> *I love those times*
> *when everything*
> *I think I know*
> *dissolves*
>
> *When the paving stones*
> *and buildings*
> *of solid assumption*
> *turn suddenly old*
> *and collapse*
>
> *And I am left newly outside*
> *in the blue shock of the biting air.*
>
> *The tumbling rush of masonry*

has stopped, but dust still flies
In wild gusts of displacement
blurring over the scene.

Later it will settle and clear
and I'll find new bearings:
a wider view, a simpler world.

The Spirit of Balance allows the energy to come through our systems, through our bodies, and allows something new to come into our being. Just breathe in the energy.

Spirit of Love
We move into the Spirit of Love, the all-encompassing Spirit of Love. We allow that to move through our system, through our body, through our whole vibrational field. We breathe in the Spirit of Love and we breathe out gratitude.

Spirit of Truth
We move to the Spirit of Truth, the wisdom within. The first differentiation of the Spirit of Love is the Spirit of Truth, which provides the design and control. We allow the old to pass away.

Spirit of Life
We move into the Spirit of Life, a further differentiation of the Spirit of Love. As it moves through us, the Spirit of Life differentiates into finer and finer expressions of the Spirit of Love. The qualities that we express have their essences before we come into the earth of our being.

Spirit of Purification
We then move into the Spirit of Purification, which allows that which is in heaven to come into our earthly being, and which prevents any distortions from moving into the heaven of ourselves. We breathe in and breathe out, allowing clarity to come through in our living.

Skeletal system
To ground our meditation, we move into our skeletal system. Envision your bones.

Breathe.

Envision your shoulders. They are an entry point into the beautiful skeletal system that gives us structure, the strength to walk, helps define who we are physically. Breathe.

Envision a diagonal line between your right shoulder and left hip. We encompass our spine, rib cage and all the organs in this area, we allow the Spirit of Love to move through.

Breathe.

Envision a diagonal line from the left shoulder to the right hip. Again, the diagonal encompasses so much. Breathe, allow the spirit of love to move through.

Breathe.

Envision the hips, the whole pelvic area. The point of gravity of our bodies is in the pelvic area. Breathe in the spirit of life. Breathe out a blessing.

Breathe.

Allow further grounding, envision a line from the right hip to the left foot. We spend so little time blessing our legs that carry us all over the world, our feet that are always in contact with the earth.

Breathe.

Envision a diagonal line from the left hip to the right foot. Allow a blessing to flow through.

Breathe.

Envision both your feet touching the earth. Feel the stability. Every step you take is blessing the earth.

Breathe.

> *The tumbling rush of masonry*
> *has stopped, but dust still flies*
> *in wild gusts of displacement*
> *blurring over the scene.*
>
> *Later it will settle and clear*
> *and I'll find new bearings:*
> *a wider view, a simpler world.*

With my feet on the ground, my world will be new.

Prayer

O Holy One, we give great thanks for being together, touching into each other, touching into ourselves, touching into the universe, and the creation that Thou hast placed us in, this beautiful, beautiful world and these beautiful connections. Amen.

JE

Walking meditation

Many meditations are conducted in a quiet place with eyes closed and attention turned inward. This one takes place outside with the eyes open. You may either walk or sit outside. The meditation promotes touching into the beauty of the outside world in resonance with the beauty within. Breathe. Relax. Open to what is around you.

Listen
Listen to the gentleness of the breeze, to the call of the birds.
Listen to the individual sounds, separate the sounds from each other.
Listen beyond hearing, listen radiantly. Listen within.

Breathe.

See
Look around you. See the various colors, so many shades of green, so many shapes.
What is ahead? Without turning, what is beside me?
See the perspective, the relationships, the proximities.
See with awe.

Breathe.

Smell
What are the aromas? Distinguish the various ones.
Are some more pleasant than others? Gentler? Stronger?
Smell with pleasure. Breathe deeply.

Breathe.

Feel
Feel the air. What is the texture? Still? Moving?
What is the temperature? Warm? Cold?

Breathe.

Feel the surface. Is it hard? Soft? Spongy? Even?
Rough? Warm? Cold?
Feel with gratitude.

Breathe.

Closing balance
Become aware of self, both inner and outer.
What is my movement? Where is my sense of being?
Allow the awareness of your surround both inner and outer to integrate into the wholeness of your being.

JE

APPENDIX

History of Attunement

Attunement is a non-touch spiritual technology, including prayer and meditation. The Attunement process allows a blessing to flow through the body via the endocrine system, bringing body, mind and heart into alignment with Spirit. When one is in alignment with Spirit, the natural result is an enhanced quality of life. One of the fundamental principles of Attunement is: "Let love radiate without concern for results." The focus is on letting, not forcing, manipulating or fixing.

Attunement was developed as a spiritual practice by Lloyd Meeker in the late 1920s. Meeker studied many esoteric and spiritual teachings and their approaches to the energetic field of the body. He determined that all truth and knowing come from within and that each of us embodies what he called the "life essences." During Attunement, it is the Life Essences, and not one's personal energy, that are shared.

In the fall of 1932, Meeker had a deeper spiritual awaking. He changed his name to Uranda and incorporated The Emissaries of Divine Light (EDL). Uranda started a community outside of Loveland, Colorado called Sunrise Ranch, as a place where the spiritual teachings could be lived and practiced.

During his teaching and travels, he met Dr. George Shears, a chiropractor, who was experimenting with no-force adjustments. Dr. Shears would hold his hands next to a patient's neck and the back would adjust itself before he touched the body. The philosophy behind the healing of chiropractic is that the Innate life force, or the God within, provides the healing. Dr. Shears and a number of chiropractors came to Sunrise Ranch for a six-month class with Uranda in 1953. Here the practice of Attunement expanded. Many chiropractic terms can be found in the teaching of Attunement.

Uranda died in 1954 and was succeeded by Martin Exeter, who emphasized the spiritual aspect of Attunement. Martin taught that when body, mind and heart are aligned with Source, healing would be a by-product.

In the 1950s, Roger de Winton expanded the teaching of Attunement to interested lay people. Roger was a mentor to both of us, Joyce and Judie, and to many of the seasoned practitioners around the globe today. Attunement continues to expand and be refined to this day.

Laurence Layne wrote a more complete history of Attunement, which is referenced in the bibliography: <u>Keepers of the Flame (1998).</u>

Endocrine glands and associated spirits

Attunement is a non-touch energy-healing practice that works primarily through the body's endocrine system. For many of the meditations in this book, we have followed the classical Attunement protocol using the endocrine system with its seven ductless glands and related spirits, beginning with the pineal or topmost gland and proceeding downwards.

A brief explanation of each gland and spirit is given here. Refer to the diagram below. For a more detailed consideration, consult our annotated bibliography.

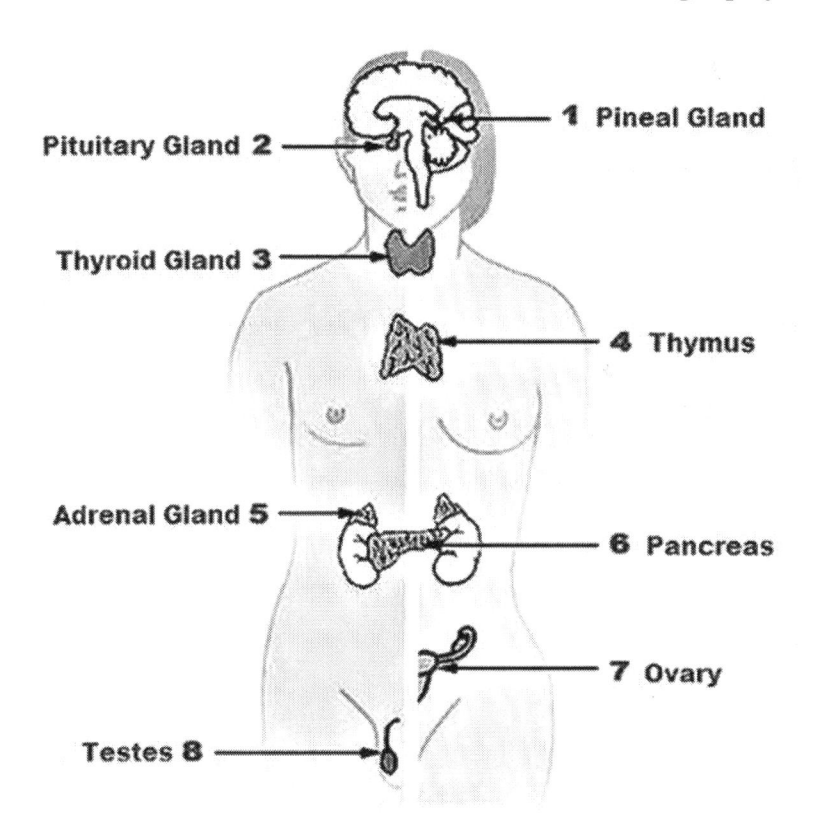

1 Pineal Gland

Pituitary Gland 2

Thyroid Gland 3

4 Thymus

Adrenal Gland 5

6 Pancreas

7 Ovary

Testes 8

Cervical pattern: The Spirit of Balance
This is where we establish an initial sense of balance in the energy field and an energetic connection with the other person or with ourselves in self-attunement or meditation. Physically, we hold our hands on each side of the neck.

Pineal: The Spirit of Love
The first or topmost endocrine gland is located in the brain. Eternal awareness originates in the pineal gland, which is the portal for the Spirit of Love to enter the body. Here is the entry point for the life force or radiant energy that vibrates at a rapid rate or high frequency. This is the purest, finest essential energy that exists.

The other six endocrine glands are differentiations of the Spirit of Love.

Pituitary: The Spirit of Truth
The pituitary gland, located between the brows, represents the spirit of the womb of truth and wisdom. This has been referred to as the "comforter" and embraces the Spirit of Love. For decades, the pituitary was regarded as the beginning point of healing processes. It is considered one of the most complex glands of the body.

This gland provides an energetic atmosphere analogous to a womb, a garden where seeds can grow and flourish. Awareness of a higher truth can appear and mental clarity is a natural result.

Thyroid: The Spirit of Life
The thyroid gland, located in the throat, controls and regulates the overall metabolism of the body and all of its internal processes. When this gland is compromised, so is the life energy flowing through the person's field. When the spiritual and physical energy are aligned, the current of life is strong.

Thymus: The Spirit of Purification
The thymus gland in the upper chest represents the Spirit of Purification and embodies the heart of being. It is the fourth opening, or midway point in the system, sometimes referred to as the crossover point. We have symbols of the Spirit of Purification in what have been called guardian angels, spirit guides, godparents, etc. On the physical level, the thymus is a major player in the immune system, keeping the self intact.

Islets of Langerhans in the Pancreas: The Spirit of Blessing
The pancreas embodies the spirit and substance of blessing. Within this structure, there are small endocrine islets. The two primary hormones they secrete are glucagon and insulin, physical representations of the sweetness of life's blessings.

Adrenals: The Spirit of the Single Eye
The adrenal glands sit on top of each kidney. They represent the singleness of purpose and the oneness of us all. These glands produce the hormone adrenaline

when we are under stress. An absence of the Spirit of Blessing can lead to feeling overwhelmed, confused and scattered. When energized, these glands allow us to be fully present, focused in the moment.

Reproductive glands or gonads: The Spirit of the New Earth
The ovaries and testes bring a further differentiation of Spirit. This is where we fully interact with the physical world. We function best when we allow stagnant, no-longer-needed energy to "compost" and fresh earth energy to strengthen and nourish us.

Annotated bibliography

Barstow, Cedar. *Right Use of Power: The Heart of Ethics.* Many Readers Publishing, 2005.

> Cedar writes about ethics as relationships that can avoid conflicts and lead to resolutions when misunderstandings occur. A must-read for anyone working in the field of energy or in the human services fields.

Henderson, Jaclyn Stein. *The Healing Power of Attunement Therapy: Stories and Practice.* Findhorn Press, 1998.

> I believe this book is out of print, but if you are able to find a used copy, it is well worth it.

Jorgensen, Chris. *Attunement Love Made Visible.* Heartland Attunement, 1996.

> This is the main book we have used in teaching Attunement. If someone is interested in practicing the art of Attunement, it is a must-read.

Jorgensen, Chris. *A Beginner's Guide to Attunement: The Energy of Being.* Heartland Attunement, 2004.

> This is helpful for people who are just entering the field of energy work. It introduces you to discerning the energy of the body.

Jorgensen, Chris. *Creator's Magic.* Heartland Attunement, 2004.

>This is a continuation and expansion of working with Attunement and the field of energy.

Layne, Laurence. *Attunement, The Sacred Landscape.* Health Light Book Publishing, 2008.

>This is an introductory guide to the world of Attunement. The book is extremely helpful to those newly acquainted with Attunement. It is also helpful for those who have been receiving attunements and want to start training to give attunements. This book is available in Spanish.

Layne, Laurence. *Keepers of the Flame: A History of Attunement.* Health Light Book Publishing, 1998.

>This companion book to Laurence's other books goes into the history of Attunement and the people who brought forward this particular sacred healing art and spiritual practice.

Layne, Laurence. *The Spiritual Nature of the Physical Body: Anatomy & Physiology for Attunement Practitioners.* Health Light Book Publishing, 2006.

>It is necessary to have a basic knowledge of the human body when one is working with energy. Laurence has a special way of making the subject

matter interesting and complete. It is a valuable tool for anyone working with the vibrational aspects of the body.

Palombo, Anthony J., D.C. *Where Spirit and Flesh Dance: Sacred Anatomy in the Fire of Creation.* Health Light Book Publishing, 2005.

> Tony sees the physical body as the angel incarnate. In reading and studying this book, you will look at yourself and others in a whole new way. Bless you, Tony.

Palombo, Anthony J., D.C. *Attunement with Sacred Sound; The Magical Use of Sound in Energy Work and Healing.* Health Book Light Publishing, 2016.

> Tony loves sound and music and is an expert in the use of sound and healing.

Shier, Andrew. *Attunement; A Way of Life.* Self-published, 2007.

> Very readable, it is a personal account of his experiences and exploration of Attunement.

Biographies

Joyce A. H. Ellenbecker, M.S.

Joyce works with energy fields and teaches a spiritual meditation and healing practice called Attunement, which includes distant and group radiation. She has been practicing Attunement since 1976 and teaching Attunement classes since 1999.

Presently, she hosts an Attunement meditation telephone call once a month and an annual Attunement retreat. She is a past member of the International Emissaries Attunement Guild and a present member of International Association of Attunement Practitioners. She is also a Level 2 Reiki practitioner.

While living at a spiritual retreat center, Joyce co-facilitated a monthly women's group and annual gathering for eight years. She also has a love of labyrinths and owns three portable ones. Previously, she was a bereavement coordinator and social worker with a hospice for seven years. She is a non-denominational minister.

Judie Arbess Diamond, B.Sc., M.A.

The foundations of Judie's life and work are energy healing, communication and music. Attunement has been a personal practice since 1982 and a professional practice for over 20 years.

Formerly a consultant for children with communication disorders, and now a teacher-practitioner of Attunement, Judie's passion is to assist people of all ages to fulfill their deepest longing for self-expression.

As a non-denominational minister, she designs and officiates at ceremonial occasions, supporting individuals, couples and families in their commitment to wholesome, respectful relationship as a basis for harmonious living. Her proudest achievement is having built and sustained healthy family relationships.

She lives with her husband, Samuel John, in a rural community in Eastern Ontario and spends considerable time in Montreal with her three adult daughters and their families.

Acknowledgements

Writing a book is never done alone or in a vacuum. Many people have been involved in bringing this book to publication. And many others have influenced us so that we could even consider doing such a project.

The beauty of acknowledging at least some of the people who impacted us is to realize the vast number, some of whom had a more direct influence than others. All were important to our learning process, whether or not they are aware of it. It would take another book to name them all.

Our Attunement development was greatly influenced by Martin Cecil Exeter, Roger de Winton, Jim Wellemeyer, Joe Antell Sr. and Chris Jorgensen. Cedar Barstow and Cliff Penwell, by their example, inspired us to become better teachers.

Tony Palombo introduced us to the Aramaic Lord's Prayer. The International Association of Attunement Practitioners, which also hosts a series of teleconferences, is an ongoing source of enrichment.

Both of us were members of the International Emissary Attunement Guild Leadership Group for over a decade and we deeply appreciate those who served on this remarkable team at various times between 1996 and 2009: Paul Price, Laurence Layne, Jude Repar, David Reis, Carol Robertson, Jean Berman, Wendy Crosman, Larry Bakur, Louise Broomberg and Tony Palombo.

We are deeply grateful for those who have come into our lives to share attunements, take classes and/or participate in retreats and other gatherings. Each event advances our understanding and clarifies aspects of the Attunement process.

A special thank you to the people who were instrumental in grounding our respective teleconferences: the original members of the Laguna Beach group, Maureen Masters, Barbara Parsons, Gaynel Rosen and Luanne Somers; Loma Huh, who did the first transcription of Joyce's recordings and Wendy Crosman for her encouragement; Wendy Zack, for prodding Judie to begin the SAFE calls, and Elsa Swyers, Lis Simpson and Nadeja Gerasimow for support in getting started. Our gratitude to those who join the teleconferences either on the phone line or in the vibrational surround.

To Adriana Palanca, kudos for your undying patience, your keen perceptions and your brilliant suggestions. The book would not be what it is without you. Martha Laing and Alexis Diamond also made invaluable contributions just when they were needed. To Laurence Layne, thank you for your openness to see this project through and your skill in getting the job done.

Finally, we wish to acknowledge our families.

Joyce — my sister, Karen, and especially my son Mark, who has traveled this territory with me.

Judie — my sister, Barbara Arbess, and my husband and daughters, John, Alexis, Samantha and Michelle Diamond for their unwavering love and support, in this, and in everything.

Made in the USA
Columbia, SC
09 March 2018